THE MEANING OF HERBS

ENGLISH CLARY, OR EYE

The Meaning of Herbs

MYTH, LANGUAGE & LORE

Gretchen Scoble

Gretchen Scoble & Ann Field

Text by Ann Fiery

Photography by Holly Lindem

CHRONICLE BOOKS

SAN FRANCISCO

To Matt, Kyle, and Nicole, for all your love and support — GS

For Clive, who continues to inspire — AF

Library of Congress Cataloging-in-Publication Data:
Scoble, Gretchen. The meaning of herbs: myth, language & lore / Gretchen Scoble and Ann Field;
text by Ann Fiery; photography by Holly Lindem.
p. cm.
ISBN 0-8118-3031-4
1. Herbs-Folklore. I. Field, Ann. II. Fiery, Ann. III. Title.
GR780.S42 2000
363'.368-dc21   00-060129
                    CIP
Printed in Hong Kong
Book and cover design by Gretchen Scoble
Calligraphy by Elvis Swift

Distributed in Canada by Raincoast Books
9050 Shaughnessy Street, Vancouver, British Columbia V6P 6E5

10 9 8 7 6 5 4 3 2 1

Chronicle Books LLC
85 Second Street
San Francisco, California 94105

www.chroniclebooks.com

Introduction

I N THE THEATER OF THE GARDEN, THE FLOWERS ARE THE
prima donnas. Brilliant and effusive, they lure us with their spec-
tacles of color and entertain us with their wanton smells. But there,
nestled next to the floral extravaganza, is the herb garden, smaller,
perhaps, and more delicately scented but carrying within it a secret
history, a lineage of magic, myth, and meaning that reaches back
through millennia to the most ancient civilizations on earth. We
all know that herbs provide us with rich and savory flavors for our
meals, heady perfumes for our gardens and homes, and homey remedies for our aches and pains, but according to ancient wisdom, herbs
were also essential for magical potions and love charms, for calling
up fairies and elves, for keeping warm or cooling down, for ensuring
immortality, for soothing the baby, for making wine.

In addition to such practical applications, each herb told a story
or held a meaning within its fragrant leaves. The bay, for example,
was worn as a crown by Apollo in honor of the lovely Daphne, who
was transformed into a bay tree as he pursued her; accordingly, the
wreath of bay leaves became the symbol of honor for Roman generals
and emperors. Like a flower, an herb tucked into a bouquet, however

inconspicuous it may look, carries with it a cache of meaning——a simple stem of chamomile suggests patience in adversity, while a sprig of verbena represents sensitivity, and rosemary is the sign of remembrance.

Treasured by the cook, beloved by the gardener, cherished by the healer, the humble herb is the practical, plain cousin of the flower——or is it? The line that demarcates herb from flower is in truth nonexistent, which is why you'll find rose, poppy, foxglove, and other constituents of the floral population in this book. Officially, an herb is defined as a plant without woody tissues, meaning, more or less, that any plant that's not a tree, bush, or shrub is an herb. More traditionally, an herb is defined by its uses: plants employed in the kitchen and the medicine chest are herbs, and plants that are merely ornamental are flowers. Of course, it was only by long——and occasionally dangerous——experimentation that the culinary or medicinal attributes of a given plant were established. Beginning in the Middle Ages, naturalists began compiling catalogues of information about herbs in order to pass along the results of that experimentation. These books, called herbals [hard "h" optional], combined all the best qualities of the cookbook, first-aid kit, advice column, gardening manual, and tall tale into one fabulous volume. In a herbal a typical entry for a given herb would include a description of the herb's behavior in the garden, instructions for using it to repel witches, a prescription for its application to various wounds, a recipe containing it, an explanation of how to make a hair tonic, and a few extra bits of general advice about life. It is on such marvelous models that we have patterned this book, including a bit of gardening lore here, a touch of cooking wisdom there, a couple of compelling remedies, and the occasional antique legend.

The herb garden has its secrets, and those who would journey along its shady paths and ancient byways will find this a useful handbook for their travels.

Coriander

[C O R I A N D R U M   S A T I V U M]

The leaf of the coriander plant constitutes an herb in its own right——cilantro, or Chinese parsley——while the seed, whole or ground, has been used in cooking for over five thousand years, making the plant as a whole extraordinarily valuable to the chef.

¶ Coriander makes an appearance in the Old Testament, where it is compared to the manna that God provided for the Israelites in their wanderings.

The seeds are used in the manufacture of gin and were mentioned in the *Arabian Nights* as having aphrodisiac qualities, but coriander is considered a witch's herb in England. Its magical reputation may stem from the fact that it has a nasty aroma until its seeds ripen, when its scent suddenly——magically——changes to a pleasant one. Perhaps this is also the source of coriander's meaning in the Victorian language of flowers: hidden merit.

Coriander is rather slow to grow and likes plenty of sun, but it will repay attention by supplying an aromatic bounty to the cook.

Parsley

[PETROSELINUM SPECIES]

The humble sprig of parsley that huddles ignominiously on restaurant plates marks a sad decline in the fortunes of this herb, which was held in such esteem by the ancient Greeks that they wreathed their victorious athletes in parsley and crowned bridesmaids with circlets of parsley and hyacinth. Parsley was dedicated to Persephone, the queen of the underworld, and parsley seed was believed to go back and forth to and from Hades nine times before sprouting, which accounts for its long germinating period. The association with the underworld made parsley an herb of death; corpses were draped in parsley garlands. The Romans were fond of parsley: they spread it on their bread for breakfast, threw parsley seeds into their fish ponds to cure sickly fish, and wore it around their necks when they went drinking to dispel intoxication.

In the middle ages, parsley was believed to be the central ingredient in the potion that witches rubbed on their brooms to make them fly. ¶ In England, parsley's ragged leaves were attributed to pixies, who tore them up as a punishment to those would replace tulip beds with the more utilitarian kitchen garden, tulips being the cradles for pixie babies.

In the language of flowers, parsley was a call for festivity.

Nettle

[URTICA DIOICA]

¶ There are a great many kinds of nettles, and nearly all of them feature stinging hairs on their leaves and stems, which accounts for their genus name, from the Latin *uro,* "I bite." Accordingly, these tall, leafy plants are commonly viewed as a garden scourge and exterminated with gusto. This antinettle sentiment is shortsighted, though, and should be reconsidered. First of all, the nettle kindly contains an antidote to its stings in the juice of its leaves, which brings rapid relief when applied to the afflicted area. Second, the nettle should be respected as one of the most ancient sources of cloth in Europe; thread made of nettle stalks antedates that of both flax and hemp and has been found in burial sites of the late Bronze Age. Third, the soldiers of the Roman Empire, finding the British winter unendurably cold, warmed themselves by chafing their skins with nettle. This may seem excessive, but it should be remembered if you find yourself without a coat in a nettle patch during a snowstorm. Fourth, nettle soup and pudding are said to be delightful [though it's the Scots who say so, and they eat haggis]. Fifth, you can make nettle beer by boiling and straining nettle tops, dandelions, goosegrass, and ginger in 4 quarts of water. Add brown sugar to taste, then place a slice of toasted bread spread with yeast on the top of the liquid, which you keep warm for 6 or 7 hours. Remove the scum from the surface, add 1 teaspoon of cream of tartar, and decant into bottles. In 6 months, you will have a tasty beer that doubles as a remedy for gout. Sixth, boiled nettle water by itself is an excellent hair conditioner.

However, it must be admitted that nettle does sting; each of those hairs conceals a cache of formic acid. All nettles should be dealt with carefully. Unsurprisingly, the meaning of the nettle in the Victorian language of flowers was cruelty.

Calendula

Calendula and *calendar* are derived from the same latin word, reflecting the plant's almost continuous blooming season. This sun-loving orange flower is also known as pot marigold, *oculus Christi,* and, amusingly enough, jackanapes on horseback.

Though it is occasionally thrown into a stewpot as an herb, and the orange petals are still sometimes used to color butter, calendula is most famous for its curative properties. The flower petals have been known for hundreds of years to provide an effective poultice for bites and stings, and the juice of the plant is available even now in ointments and lotions for chapped or burned skin. During the Civil War, both the Northern and Southern armies used calendula to bind up wounds. ¶ In Mexico, however, calendula is called the flower of death because it is believed to have sprung up from the blood of natives killed by the Spanish invaders, and it is used to adorn gravestones on the Day of the Dead.

Strangely, the marigold is the symbol of mental anguish in flower language.

Ginseng

[PANAX GINSENG {ASIA},
PANAX QUINQUEFOLIUS {NORTH AMERICA}]

¶ The root of the ginseng plant is regarded as an omnipotent healer in China, where there are a number of legends about its origins, including the belief that the herb grew when lightning struck a clear stream. According to Chinese herbalists, ginseng is a lifelong cure-all, treating baby colic at one end of the spectrum and mitigating the depredations of age at the other. It is believed to improve the mental powers as well as the physical, extend the life span, and increase the libido——all at the same time.

The ginseng plant attains a height of a mere twelve inches, but that achievement takes six to seven years, and the plant extracts so many minerals and nutrients from the soil that the earth in which it grows is exhausted and requires a decade to recover. As a result, ginseng was for many years in extremely limited supply and terrifically expensive in China and other East Asian countries. In the eighteenth century, wild ginseng was found in Canada and exported to China, where it was sold for many times its weight in silver. Once cultivated only for export to Asia, North American ginseng is now consumed in the West in teas and powders as a remedy for insomnia and general debilitation.

Lavender

[LAVANDULA SPECIES]

The aroma of lavender, at once delicate and invigorating, is among the world's most beloved. Lavender is native to the Mediterranean region, and though there are many varieties of the herb, the most highly scented, *Lavandula angustfolia,* is the most difficult to grow, as it prefers altitudes of 2,000 to 5,000 feet. Common lavender, *L. officinalis,* is a more docile plant, growing happily at a more reasonable 1,500 feet, and is widely planted in France, Italy, and England. In France alone over 700 tons of distilled lavender essence are produced each year.

It's no wonder——the lovely smell of lavender has been treasured for centuries, beginning with the ancient Romans, who used lavender to perfume their baths and so derived its name from *lavare,* "to wash." ¶ There is an old legend that lavender received its scent from the baby Jesus: when Mary washed his swaddling clothes, she hung them out to dry on a silvery lavender bush, and ever since, the smell of heaven has lingered on the plant.

Still employed for medicinal purposes, the flowers were once boiled in water to create a headache tonic and added to wine to soothe the "swooning of the heart." Modern-day aromatherapists recommend lavender to ease tension and relieve fatigue.

In the language of flowers, lavender symbolized mistrust.

21ᵉ LEÇON. — LES NOBLES ET LE PEUPLE

61. Sous le régime féodal on appelait nobles tous les seigneurs. Ils avaient des châteaux forts, des guerriers, et ils étaient les maîtres de tous les habitants de leurs domaines.

62. Le peuple comprenait les vilains [1] et les serfs.

63. Les vilains étaient les artisans [2] et les cultivateurs libres.

64. Les serfs étaient les cultivateurs non libres. Les serfs étaient attachés à la glèbe, c'est-à-dire à la terre qu'ils cultivaient : ils ne pouvaient la quitter et ils changeaient de maître en même temps qu'elle.

Un château féodal.

RÉCIT. — Le château féodal

1. Le château du seigneur se dressait ordinairement sur une colline élevée.

2. C'était un édifice vaste et sombre, entouré de larges fossés et de hautes murailles flanquées [3] de tours.

3. Un *pont-levis* [4], établi en face de la porte principale, permettait de franchir le fossé ; mais, à l'approche

de l'ennemi, on relevait ce pont contre la porte, au moyen de chaînes.

4. Au milieu de la cour intérieure, s'élevait une grosse tour appelée *donjon*, fortifiée par des tourelles, et entourée d'un fossé à pont-levis. C'est dans le donjon que le seigneur gardait ce qu'il avait de plus précieux.

5. Les cabanes des vilains et des serfs se groupaient autour du château féodal, bâti surtout pour servir de refuge aux populations contre la fureur des Normands.

6. Un *guetteur* [5] veillait nuit et jour au haut du donjon, pour observer la campagne. Si l'ennemi apparaissait au loin, le guetteur sonnait du cor ; aussitôt les hommes d'armes se préparaient à la défense, et les paysans, abandonnant leurs travaux, couraient chercher un asile auprès du seigneur.

7. Lorsque la première enceinte [6] était forcée par l'ennemi, les défenseurs du château se retiraient dans le donjon, et, quand tout espoir était perdu, ils s'évadaient par de longs souterrains conduisant ordinairement dans une forêt du voisinage.

Explication des mots.

1. **Vilains** : les vilains furent ainsi appelés parce qu'ils habitaient des maisons de campagne ou fermes nommées *villas*. — 2. **Artisans** : ceux qui ont un métier manuel, comme les charpentiers, les cordonniers... — 3. **Murailles flanquées** de tours : murailles fortifiées par des tours bâties sur leurs flancs ou côtés, de distance en distance. — 4. **Pont-levis** : pont qu'on peut lever à volonté. — 5. **Guetteur** : celui qui guette, qui surveille du haut d'une tour ou d'un clocher. — 6. **Enceinte** : muraille qui entourait le château ; quelques châteaux forts avaient deux et même trois enceintes.

Questionnaire.— *Leçon.* — 61. Qui appelait-on nobles ou seigneurs sous le régime féodal ? — 62. Que comprenait le peuple ? — 63. Qui appelait-on vilains ? — 64. Que savez-vous des serfs ? — *Récit.* — 1. Où se dressait le château du seigneur ? — 2. Dé-crivez le château du seigneur. — 3. Parlez du pont-levis. — 4. Qu'était-ce que le donjon. — 5. Où étaient les cabanes des vilains et des serfs ? — 6. Que faisait le guetteur ? — 7. Que faisaient les assiégés lorsque la première enceinte était forcée ?

Devoir. — Dites ce que vous savez du donjon et du guetteur.

Cloves

[E U G E N I A   C A R Y O P H Y L L A T A]

The dried seeds we call cloves are harvested from the tree of the same name, an evergreen native of the Spice Islands that is such an avid consumer of water that nothing else can grow near it. Cloves have been put to medicinal and culinary use for millennia; they were particularly popular in medieval Europe for their strong scent.

Our Christmas tradition of decorating oranges with patterns of cloves to create an aromatic pomander dates back to Renaissance England. ¶ Clove is a critical element in many holiday treats, from cakes and cookies to pies and punch; medicinally, it remedies a malady brought on by an overabundance of these tasty desserts——oil of clove is a common cure for toothache.

Nasturtium

[TROPAEOLUM MAJUS]

Cheerful nasturtium, which now grows uncontrollably in most sunny climates, was once accounted an extremely rare and elegant plant. Native to the Americas, it took the Old World by storm when it was brought back by the early explorers. ¶ Nasturtium's generic name *Tropaeolum* is latin for "trophy," which evolved from an old legend that the plant grew from the blood of a dying Trojan warrior. Perhaps this tale is the source of the flower's symbolic meaning of patriotism.

With its delicate scent and vibrant red, orange, and yellow flowers, nasturtium is a splendid garden flower, though it tends to invade all nooks and crannies when left to its own devices. Nasturtium leaves and seeds are eaten in some parts of the world, and the peppery flower petals can be found sprinkled generously over salads in restaurants that advocate complete garden consumption.

Ginger

[ZINGIBER OFFICINALE]

A native of Asia, ginger is now grown throughout the tropics and in the Americas. This exotic, heat-loving plant grows to a height of three to four feet and bears glamorous white, yellow, and purple flowers, but it is the dull brown root, or rhizome, that is most treasured. Its delightfully spicy aroma has become the scent of Christmas, and its pungent, warming taste is essential to such favorite desserts as gingerbread as well as being a key ingredient in all sorts of delicious curries, drinks, and vegetable dishes.

A major trade item between Europe and Asia for centuries, ginger was much revered in the West for its curative properties. ¶ Because the rhizome has the shape of the human digestive tract, early medicos assumed that it was a remedy for stomach disorders; coincidentally——and luckily for their patients——it is. Employed as an aphrodisiac by Madame du Barry, it was said to drive even the sluggish Louis XV to the heights of lust.

Echinacea

[ECHINACEA ANGUSTIFOLIA]

¶ The Native Americans of the Great Plains were the first to discover the manifold benefits of echinacea. This charming purple flower was valued as a remedy for a number of maladies, including stomachache, headache, snakebites, scrapes, and itches. Also known as purple coneflower and black sampson, echinacea was hailed in Europe as a New World cure-all and in the seventeenth century became an exceedingly rare and expensive medicinal herb.

Today echinacea has achieved new popularity as an immune system stimulant. Taken at the first sign of a cold, it acts as a call to arms for your natural defenses and fortifies the barriers against viral organisms. If the cold has already taken hold, echinacea will at least shorten its duration.

Tarragon

[ARTEMISIA DRACUNCULUS]

One of the more benign members of the wormwood family, tarragon grows in tapering spires with narrow, waving green leaves. Native to southern Europe, it prefers dry soil and plenty of sunshine. ¶ Until recently tarragon enjoyed little esteem; the medieval herbalists had no regard for it, and its use in the kitchen was dismissed as a French quirk. Now it is one of the supreme herbs of the kitchen garden, its rich, distinctive flavor an essential component of such necessities as bernaise sauce and ravigote dressing.

Though the word *tarragon* itself seems to have an Arabic past, its specific name, *dracunculus,* meaning "little dragon," is derived from the serpentine shape of its roots. Early medicos, who correlated an herb's appearance with its application, used tarragon as an antidote to snakebite, but modern-day herbalists suggest that chewing a leaf of tarragon will cure hiccups.

Artisans, artists,
from the painters of Lascaux, 30,000 years ago,
to the French painters of today,
from the Gallic artisans to artisans everywhere,
in every field, the French are faithful
to the tradition of beautiful workmanship.

Embroidery workshop.

Mustard

[B R A S S I C A   N I G R A ,   B R A S S I C A   A L B A]

Though there are many species of mustard, two have pride of place in the kitchen: black mustard and white mustard [the latter is sometimes called hedge mustard]. They look very much the same, both having yellow flowers, but the seeds of the former are black and smaller. What we find in our jars of mustard is usually a combination of the two, colored with turmeric, since mustard prepared directly from the seed is an "unmustardlike" brown. ¶ White mustard grows wildly in many parts of world, whereas black mustard is more selective, but both are ancient herbs, mentioned in the Bible and lauded by the Greek physician Asclepius.

Mustard seed, pounded together with vinegar, was a popular condiment in the Middle Ages, when it was eaten "with any grosse meates." However, it went out of style in the more refined seventeenth century. As one herbalist wrote loftily in 1640, "Our ancient forefathers, even the better sort . . . were not sparing in the use hereof . . . but nowadays it is seldome used by their successors, being accounted the clownes sauce, and therefore not fit for their tables."

The mustard plaster is a fine old remedy for aches and pains and removing splinters. Mix 1 part mustard to 4 parts whole-wheat flour and enough warm water to make a paste. Spread it onto a cloth and apply to the injury, taking care not to leave the plaster on too long, for blistering can occur. The herbalist Nicholas Culpeper thought mustard would cure pretty much everything, from poisoning and heart ailments to baldness and cricks in the neck.

012 ROMA - Venere Capitolina (Museo Capitolino)

ROMA · Museo Capitolino · Vaso Egiziano

Laurus nobilis

[L A U R U S   N O B I L I S]

¶ The bay is the most illustrious member of the laurel family, for the beauteous Daphne was transformed into a bay as she fled from the lascivious clutches of Apollo. In her honor Apollo twisted a bay branch into a crown and wore it ever afterward, which was the source of the laurel wreath that crowned victorious Roman generals and emperors. Its association with great deeds and exalted heroes gave rise to the bay leaf's Victorian meaning: "I change but in death." Today, both the poet laureate and the lazy fellow who is merely "resting upon his laurels" are garnished, in one way or another, with bay leaf. Likewise, anyone who has received a bachelor's degree has been decorated, if only etymologically, with bay leaves and berries [*bacca-laureus*].

In ancient times the pungent scent of bay gave rise to the persistent idea that the plant dispelled contagion. In 1629 a dire sense of foreboding fell over the Italian city of Padua when the bay trees bordering its university mysteriously withered and died; unprotected, the city was soon struck with bubonic plague.

Culpeper, the great seventeenth-century medico, wrote that bay "resisteth witchcraft very potently," which may be the source of the British custom of placing a pot of bay at the door to ward off spells and curses. A bay tree, grown in a pot, is not only useful for seasoning soups and stuffings but is also believed to prevent your house from being struck by lightning.

Vervain

Even if it is not much in use today, vervain must be respected for its marvelous past. ¶ This weedy, wavering plant, ornamented with tiny pink or purple flowers, was a sacred herb of the Druids, who used it in spells and divinatory rituals as well as in magical medicines and incense. River water steeped with vervain became a purifying bath, and the juice of vervain was mixed into their sacramental wine. According to ancient texts, the herb had to "be gathered about the rising of the dog-star, but so as neither sun nor moon be at that time above the earth to see it." It was necessary, after uprooting the vervain, to make amends to the earth by offering her a honeycomb "for the wrong and violence done in depriving her of so holy a herb."

The invading Romans seem to have taken a leaf from the Druidical book, for in the first century, vervain began to appear in Roman temples, as well. Little brooms made of vervain were used to sweep the altars and dust the statues. Dedicated to Venus, vervain was also important in marriage rituals; the Roman bride picked sprigs of vervain on her wedding morning to guarantee a happy union. In battles vervain was worn by messengers as a symbol of diplomatic immunity, rather like a flag of truce or a red cross today.

Vervain has a place in Christian legend, as well. It was believed to grow at the foot of the Cross. It was thus considered to provide security against witches, though some commentators claimed that the witches themselves used vervain in their potions. A recipe for a love potion that has come down through the ages would seem to support the latter: in an oven, heat vervain, seeds and flowers of elecampane, and mistletoe berries until they are brittle and dry. Pound them into a powder and put a teaspoonful into a glass of wine for your beloved. You will instantly be loved in return.

Vervain fell out of use after the Middle Ages, though in the seventeenth century, Nicholas Culpeper suggested that applied together with oil of roses and vinegar, vervain "easeth inveterate pains and aching of the head, and is good for those that are frantick."

In a bouquet vervain suggests enchantment.

Yarrow

[ACHILLEA MILLEFOLIUM]

A pretty flower with plentiful, lacy leaves, yarrow has also been known as knyghten milfoil or soldier's woundwort for its healing properties. There is a legend that the Greek hero Achilles tended his wounded men with yarrow after learning of the herb's magic properties from Chiron, his tutor in medicine, music, and hunting. ¶ In France yarrow is known as *herbe au charpentier,* presumably because it was used to remedy the hurts caused by the sharp tools of the carpenter.

Though yarrow's bitter leaves were occasionally used in brewing beer, it is now of little use in the kitchen. However, country wisdom has it that yarrow carried in a bridal bouquet ensures seven years of happiness, and that is certainly better than a dish of soup.

If you receive yarrow in a bouquet, beware: it signifies war.

Rue

[R U T A G R A V E O L E N S]

Rue is a useful herb, warding off fleas, flies, plagues, and witches.
¶ In fact, it has a generally disinfectant nature, which
accounts for the tradition of a rue bouquet being given
to a judge as he entered his courtroom, in order to coun-
teract the germs that lurked on the criminals. Brushes of
rue were used to sprinkle holy water in the celebration of the Mass,
giving it the nickname *herb of grace.* During a plague in Marseilles,
thieves used a vinegar infused with rue to protect themselves against
any sickness that might be dwelling in the houses they robbed; hence,
the "vinegar of the four thieves" became a noted cleanser and disinfectant.

Rue has strong connections to magic and witches, who were
believed to use the herb in creating magic circles and spells.
Strangely, rue was also considered a witch antidote, so bunches of
rue were hung at doors to keep witches from entering. In addition
to acting as a talisman against the evil eye, rue eaten at bedtime
prevented the guilty from talking in their sleep.

Native to southeastern Europe, rue grows in small shrubs with
bluish gray leaves and yellow flowers. Never plant it near mint, as
these two herbs do not get along.

For the Victorians, rue was the sign of
disdain.

Chives

¶ The daintiest member of the onion family, chives are an essential element in any kitchen garden. Both the stalks and the flowers of chives may be used as a flavoring, though you must pick between the two, for the only way to maintain edible stalks is to pinch off the flowers when they appear. In addition to providing a delicate, savory touch to all types of dishes, chives are a beneficial companion plant in the garden; such strange bedfellows as carrots and roses are linked by their grateful acceptance of chives as neighbor.

Overworked in the kitchen, chives are unemployed in the medicine chest. They have virtually no medical uses, and what's more, the herbalist Culpeper wrote that "If they be eaten raw they send up very hurtful vapours into the brain." On the other hand, there is an old British tradition that a border of chives around a flower bed keeps the evil spirits out of the garden. A cluster of chive leaves hung over the doorway was thought to have an equally protective effect in the house.

Scotch Thistle

[ONOPORDUM ACANTHIUM]

The Scotch thistle, which sports a soft, downy cap of purple atop a tall, thorn-covered spire, is a model of vigorous self-defense: should the unsuspecting reach for the beguiling crown, he will be violently stung by the prickles. ¶ The plant is known as the Scotch thistle because it became the emblem of beleaguered Scotland during the Danish invasions of the tenth century. A marauding Dane, sneaking by an encampment of sleeping Scottish soldiers, stepped on a thistle and let out a scream that roused the entire army, which proceeded to rout the interlopers. The royal House of Stuart, which admittedly had good cause to be defensive, adopted the thistle in its standard, accompanied by the motto *Nemo me impune lacesset,* "No one injures me with impunity."

As is proper for such an antagonistic plant, the Scotch thistle grows happily in inhospitable soils and inappropriate places. It may be cultivated in the garden for its lovely purple flower and its imposing presence, but the gardener may find it impossible to control once it takes root.

In a bouquet the Scotch thistle announces the desire for retaliation.

Garlic

[ALLIUM SATIVUM]

¶ This pungent member of the onion family is so ancient that its origins are lost in the sands of time, but it is known to have been a favorite food of the ancient Egyptians, who believed that it was divine. In China, Japan, and Turkey, it was held to have magical powers and worn as a talisman; likewise, the Greeks set it at crossroads to placate the witch Hecate. There is an Islamic legend that garlic sprang up in the Devil's footprints as he stalked out of the Garden of Eden. In western Europe garlic dispels evil spirits that come from beneath the earth, and in the Balkans wards off vampires, who, as we all know, may be controlled by waving a clove of garlic near their faces.

Its medical applications are manifold. The juice of the garlic bulb contains an antibiotic and, diluted in water, can be applied directly to cuts. Taken in capsule form, garlic protects against colds and may provide benefit to cancer sufferers. An old country remedy for whooping cough was to place a garlic bulb in the toe of the patient's stocking. Nicholas Culpeper wrote that garlic was "anciently accounted the poor man's treacle, it being a remedy for all diseases and hurts [except those which itself breeds]."

Strawberry

[FRAGARIA SPECIES]

Strawberry may well be the perfect plant. It is charming to look at, with its delicate white flowers and crimson fruits hanging like glowing lanterns among neat green leaves. It produces deliciously sweet berries, which may be sauced, jammed, juiced, or simply and happily popped into the mouth fresh off the stem. It has a light, distinctive fragrance that provokes nostalgia and delight. In addition to all these virtues, the leaves and fruit of the plant hold remedies for a variety of ills.

The strawberry got its name through its wandering habits, being a "stray-berry." Wild strawberry will spread into nooks and crannies, provided it receives abundant water. Domestic varieties are less inclined to stray, but they too need plenty of water and soil that drains well. There are numerous varieties of strawberry, including at least nine that are native to North America. ¶ Native Americans used strawberry in breads and as a cure for stomachache, and the early settlers took the hint, producing strawberry wine and cordial.

The strawberry leaf is featured on the traditional crowns of dukes, earls, and marquises. In a completely unconnected tradition, strawberries are deemed great aphrodisiacs, probably due as much to the sensuality of biting into the tempting fruit as to any lusty chemicals it holds.

Appropriately, the meaning of the strawberry in the language of flowers is "perfect excellence."

Thyme

[THYMUS SPECIES]

Together with basil and rosemary, thyme forms the great herbal triumvirate. The rich, woody aroma of thyme improves everything it comes in contact with——pasta dishes, vegetables, roasted meats and potatoes. As an added benefit, it is quite easy to grow, needing little more than abundant sunshine and fairly dry soil. Bees adore thyme, and in Greece, where thyme grows wild over the hills, the hives produce thyme honey, a great delicacy.

Thyme lawns were once quite popular, though the herb was not nearly as comfortable as grass for a shady nap. Thyme has a scent thought to provoke courage and strength. Accordingly, it became a symbol of bravery, and medieval noblewomen embroidered thyme leaves on the scarves their knights wore at tournaments.

Thyme was also considered a death herb. In England there was a legend that the souls of murdered men rest in thyme flowers, and in Wales the herb is planted on graves. ¶ More cheerfully, thyme was a charm for seeing fairies. You simply collected thyme flowers from a hillside where the fairies were known to gather and laid the flowers upon your eyelids. Then you would have the power to see any fairy who happened to be nearby.

The name *thyme* comes from a Greek word meaning "fumigate," and the herb is a great refresher of body and soul. Thyme added to the bath gives off a scent that invigorates the bather, and the soldier's tradition of a thyme bath before battle is probably the source of the herb's meaning in the language of flowers: a call to action.

Evening Primrose

[OENOTHERA BIENNIS]

Dreamy gardeners of eras past sometimes created special moonlight gardens of flowers that love the night. Chief among these is the evening primrose, whose shimmering pastel petals begin to open at twilight and whose delicate perfume beckons the restless out into the garden for a nighttime stroll. Perhaps because its nocturnal allure is betrayed by its nondescript daytime guise, in floral language the evening primrose is the symbol of inconstancy.

The evening primrose is not really a primrose at all, and as befits such a mysterious, shadowy plant, it has many aliases: night willow herb, large rampion, fever plant, king's cure-all, and scurvish. ¶ A New World plant, evening primrose was a valuable source of pain medicine for Native Americans and is still used by herbalists as an antianxiety treatment. Despite its delicate appearance, evening primrose grows well in meager or dry soil.

Rosemary

[ROSMARINUS OFFICINALIS]

Rosemary has been a significant herb since antiquity; together with ivy, myrtle, and bay, it was one of the most common plants in the Roman garden. Rosemary prospers in temperate climates cooled by sea breezes; its name come from the Latin words *ros* and *maris,* meaning "spray of the sea." The herb grows well in pots because the constriction of the roots keeps its fragrance strong. It is also a dependable delight in the garden, where it can grow up to eight feet, though there is an old English legend that rosemary "passeth not commonly in highte the highte of Criste whill he was a man on Erthe" and that a bush will not grow taller after its thirty-third year, the age of Christ at his death. Rosemary sports light blue or white flowers that are extremely appealing to bees.

¶ In the Middle Ages, students were encouraged to twine sprigs of rosemary through their hair to stimulate their brains; consequently, the herb has come to be associated with remembrance, most famously by Ophelia in *Hamlet,* "There's rosemary, that's for remembrance——pray you, love, remember." Perhaps as a corollary, rosemary was a part of funeral rites throughout the ages. Branches of rosemary were placed in the hands of the dead; occasionally, these branches took root, and there are some references to disinterred coffins containing corpses entwined with rosemary.

The herb has also had a role at wedding ceremonies throughout the ages. Greek and Roman couples wore wreaths of rosemary on their wedding days. In the seventeenth century, gilded sprigs of rosemary were distributed to guests as wedding favors. Country bridal bouquets often included a bit of rosemary as a charm for a happy marriage.

A rosemary tonic was sold by apothecaries to remedy "affections of the head caused by wine"——that is, hangovers——and leaves of rosemary were often added to baths to calm the nerves and clear the head. Oil of rosemary may aid those suffering from migraine, and rosemary shampoos are thought to make the hair shine. Placed in the clothes chest, rosemary will repel moths.

In addition to remembrance, rosemary says, "Your presence revives me" in the language of flowers.

Cardamom

[ELETTARIA CARDAMOMUM]

Cardamom was considered a powerful aphrodisiac in earlier eras; for example, in sixteenth-century Arabia, Sheik Nefzawi, redoubtable author of *The Perfumed Garden,* a collection of sexual advice and tall tales, suggested that a combination of cinnamon, cloves, nutmeg, pepper, chrysanthemum, gillyflowers, and cardamom, taken morning and night, would render the imbiber invincible. Less dramatically, cardamom seeds were also used to freshen the breath in India and added to coffee in Arabic countries to stimulate conviviality. ¶ In Europe there is a tradition that cardamom is much in favor with witches for poisons and love philters.

Dandelion

[TARAXACUM OFFICINALE]

The bane of gardeners everywhere, the dandelion is egregiously abundant due to its overly efficient method of broadcasting its seeds. The plant has many unappreciated virtues, though: the leaves are good to eat in salads and may also be dried and ground up for a coffee substitute. The bright yellow flower heads make a light-tasting wine. Peculiarly, the entire plant yields a vibrant magenta dye. Dandelion is such a splendid diuretic that its common name in France is *pisenlit.*

Dandelions are a useful divinatory tool, as well. A girl who wants to know whether her sweetheart is thinking of her has merely to blow on a dandelion puff three times. If any seed stalks remain, that is proof positive that she is in his thoughts. Indeed, in the Victorian language of flowers, the dandelion is called the rustic oracle.

¶ The name of the plant comes from the early French *dent de leon,* meaning "lion's tooth," undoubtedly a reference to the jagged edges of the leaves. In some far-flung regions of England, it is called devil's milk pail.

Rose

[ROSA SPECIES]

The rose may be the only flower whose symbolism is still widely known: the rose always has and always will represent love. The rose and love have been inextricably mixed since classical times, when the flower was associated with the goddess of love and beauty, Venus. ¶ According to legend, the first roses were thornless. Venus' son, Cupid, was smelling a rose, when a bee emerged from the flower and stung him on the lip. To placate him, Venus strung his bow with bees, first removing their stingers, which she placed on the rose stem instead. In another story, all roses were white until Venus tore her foot on a briar and dyed the roses red with her blood.

In Christian lore the rose's red color comes from Christ's blood, and in the Middle Ages, the Mystic Rose was the symbol of Mary. Dante borrowed the rose image for his *Paradiso,* in which the empyrean realm of heaven is structured like a giant white rose, with beatified souls arranged on its petals.

Under the symbols of the red rose and the white rose, the English Houses of Lancaster and York battled for some thirty years in a slaughter of such magnitude that by the end there was neither a Lancaster nor York left to ascend the throne. The sole survivor on the field, Henry Tudor, renamed the red rose the Tudor rose and made it a symbol of his rule.

It's well known that the rose lends its scent to myriad perfumes and lotions and oils, but the less known medicinal uses of the rose are also manifold. Rose water was thought in the sixteenth century to strengthen the heart, and it is still prescribed for this purpose by modern-day herbalists. Rose hips boiled into a syrup were found by the early American settlers to be efficacious against itches. Today rose hips are known to be a rich source of vitamin C, and rose hip pills and teas are used to prevent colds and coughs.

Even in the kitchen, roses have a place. Rose water adds a delicious aroma to Moroccan and Indian dishes, and crystallized rosebuds are an epicurean adornment to a birthday cake. Queen Victoria partook of rose petal sandwiches at tea. These can be made by discarding the white points of any sweet-smelling rose petals and daintily placing the remaining petals in a single layer on a crustless piece of buttered bread. Cap with another buttered slice of bread sans crust and serve with rose tea.

Though the rose in general means love, different roses have specific messages as well. A white rose announces, "I am worthy of you." A yellow rose signifies decrease of love or jealousy. A Christmas rose says, "Tranquilize my anxiety," and a thornless rose represents early attachment. A full-blown rose placed over two buds indicates secrecy, and a rose leaf without an accompanying bud suggests, "You may hope."

Savory

[S ATUREIA HORTENSIS, S ATUREIA MONTANA]

Both summer savory and winter savory have vivid, peppery-tasting leaves that enliven soups, sandwiches, and fish dishes, and both have the pleasing characteristic of growing well in dry and rocky soil. Both feature purple flowers and were once considered to be herbs of the satyrs and therefore conducive to lust. ¶ **Pregnant women were forbidden to eat savory of either ilk.** The juice of both savories was used by medieval ladies as a bleach for tanned skin.

There is very little difference between the two herbs, except that summer savory is a beneficial companion plant for beans, and winter savory isn't.

Basil

[O c i m u m   b a s i l i c u m]

Greek botanists believed basil to be poisonous; the ancient Romans,
on the other hand, believed that the smell of basil inspired love.
Thus, a woman seeking true love needed merely to hand the object
of her affections a sprig of basil, and he would be hers forever.
Likewise, a pot of basil on a Roman woman's balcony was a sign that
her lover should scale the walls with dispatch. Given these opposing
classical viewpoints, the seventeenth-century herbalist Nicholas
Culpeper was confounded: "As it helps the deficiency of Venus in
one kind, so it spoils all her action in another. I dare write no more
of it," he concluded mysteriously.

¶ Native to India, basil is a sacred herb in the Hindu
tradition, often grown in pots near temples and houses.
In burial ceremonies, a basil leaf is placed on the dead to
ensure that the gates of heaven will open for them. In
Egypt, too, the leaves are scattered on graves. In the Western tradition, basil has more earthly connotations: in Crete the herb signifies
"love washed in tears," and in Italy its folk name is *kiss-me, Nicholas.*
In medieval England basil was thought to be a surefire cure for obesity
in women [not in men, for some reason]. You simply place a sprig of
basil under each dish, making sure that your intended subject doesn't
notice, and "she will eat none of that which is in the Dish."

John Keats immortalized basil in his poem "Isabella, or the Pot
of Basil," in which the lover of Isabella is murdered by her jealous

brothers. The grief-stricken girl retrieves her lover's head and hides it in a pot of basil, which she keeps by her side and waters with her tears. When her gruesome secret is discovered by the brothers, they steal the pot, and Isabella dies of grief.

Despite the Greeks' antipathy for basil, its name comes from the Greek word for "royal," *basilikon*. A perennial in warm climates, basil is easy to grow and thrives in containers. Its small white flowers should be ruthlessly pruned in order to induce vigorous growth of the tasty leaves. There is an ancient Roman tradition that a gardener planting basil must curse and insult it in order to make the herb flourish.

According to some Victorian handbooks on the language of flowers, basil symbolized the sender's need for the recipient's good wishes. In starker manuals the herb simply meant hatred.

Agrimony

¶ The Greek word from which agrimony is derived, *argemóné,* indicates that this herb was used to relieve eye troubles, but for the Anglo-Saxons, agrimony was primarily a talisman against goblins and other intransigent supernatural beings. It is also called church steeples for its graceful spires of yellow flowers, and cocklebur and sticklewort for its tenacious burs.

Oregano and Sweet Marjoram

Oregano is the fraternal twin of sweet marjoram, as is revealed by their shared genus name, *Origanum*. ¶ Derived from the Greek *oras,* meaning "mountain," and *ganos,* meaning "joy," the oregano family is the Joy of the Mountain. These herbs grow wild in the mountains of the Mediterranean region, and their pleasant smell and delightful flavor bring joy to those who use them. In the United States, marjoram and oregano are considered two different herbs, but in Europe the names are used interchangeably.

The Greeks believed that oregano was created by Aphrodite herself, and Greek women used the herb as a perfume. Early herbalists prescribed oregano to those who "are given to overmuch sighing," and enraged bears were believed to calm themselves by chewing on oregano bushes. Likewise, oregano tonic is given to cows after calving to calm their nerves. An infusion of oregano is a sure cure for seasickness. In the German countryside, marjoram was often hung over the door to protect against any spells that might have been cast on the dwelling by witches.

Nowadays the aromatic leaves of oregano and marjoram are used mostly in cooking, lending their rich scent to meats, stews, and soups. Both are common herbs, easily grown, even to the point of becoming weeds in some mountainous localities. Indeed, the state of Oregon was named for the profusion of oregano that grew wild there. Sweet marjoram symbolized happiness in the Victorian language of flowers, and in Germany a bouquet of the herb was the sign of a light heart.

Foxglove

[DIGITALIS PURPUREA]

Named for the glovelike shape of its hanging flowers, foxglove is native to England, where it grows in wild, spiraling curls along shady roads and provides brilliant towers of purple and white in more formal gardens. ¶ Because foxglove was unknown to the ancients, it was believed by European physicians to have no medicinal value until the eighteenth century, when the plant was discovered to be the source of digitalis, a medicine that slows the heart and is still widely used in treating heart disease. Except in minute doses, digitalis is deadly poison, and, accordingly, foxglove is known in Ireland as dead man's thimbles. However, weak tea of foxglove flowers, taken in great quantities, was a cheap alternative to alcohol in rural areas of England. In Wales a black dye made from foxglove leaves was painted in crosses on doorsteps; apparently, it kept witches at bay.

In the language of flowers, the foxglove represents insincerity, perhaps because its charming looks disguise its poisonous properties.

Bergamot

[MONARDA DIDYMA, CITRUS BERGAMIA]

Also known as Oswego tea and bee balm, fragrant bergamot flowers of the *Monarda* genus make a tasty, lemony tea. ¶ Dried and ground to a powder, the flowers were used as a "headache snuff" by early American healers. A swamp plant, bergamot is difficult to grow, but it rewards the gardener by attracting bees to the shady spots it prefers. Some early beekeepers recommended rubbing hives with bergamot to keep the bees from straying.

Oil of bergamot, which is used in perfumes——and, incidentally, in Earl Grey tea——comes from the fruit of a different plant altogether, *Citrus bergamia*. In Edwardian England dried bergamot fruit was combined with lemon verbena, geranium leaves, thyme, mint, lavender, rosemary, and southernwood and placed in sachets, which were hung from chairs to scent parlors in the winter. The smell of bergamot is thought by modern aromatherapists to alleviate tension and anxiety.

Poppy

[PAPAVER SPECIES]

The poppy comes in many varieties, some merely pretty, like the Alpine and Iceland poppies; some steeped in history, like the Flanders poppy, which grew in profusion on the battlefields of World War I; some glamorous, like the massive Oriental poppy; and one wicked and dangerous, the opium poppy, whose sap is harvested for opium and morphine.

¶ The legend of the poppy begins with Proserpina, who was borne off to Hades by Pluto, the god of the underworld. Her mother, Ceres, wild with grief, traveled throughout Sicily in search of her daughter. As night fell she was climbing the rocky heights of Mount Etna, and a few sympathetic gods, unable to return her daughter to her, sent thousands of poppies to bloom on the sides of the mountain; their petals, glowing red, lit her way. The sorrowful Ceres plucked a few flowers and tasted their seeds; overcome by narcotic languor, she lay down and slept among the poppies. Several millennia later, Dorothy did the same thing in *The Wizard of Oz*.

The poppy represents both oblivion and fantastic extravagance in the language of flowers.

Borage

[BORAGO OFFICINALIS]

With its distinctive star shape and intense blue color, borage is
among the most attractive of herbs, at least until the end of its growing season, when the soft hairs that deck the leaves become stringy,
pesky prickles. Flowering in the summer, borage makes a desirable
companion plant. It deters tomato hornworms when set down next
to tomato plants, and near strawberries its presence ensures prolific
fruit.

¶ The early English herbalist Culpeper suggested
borage as a remedy for "pensiveness and melancholy,"
and there is an old country adage, "Take borage for
courage," that finds support in modern studies showing that the
chemicals in the herb act upon the adrenal gland. This may also
have some bearing on its meaning in the Victorian language of
flowers: abruptness.

Borage must always be used fresh in the kitchen, never dried.
The leaves, with a light cucumber-like taste, can be added to sandwiches or salads. For the budding scientist, borage flowers have the
interesting property of turning bright pink when hot vinegar is
poured upon them.

Mint

[M E N T H A   S P E C I E S]

¶ In all its varieties, mint is named after the Greek water nymph Minthe, who was changed into the herb by the jealous goddess Proserpina when Pluto cast lustful looks her way. Some time later mint was dedicated to the Virgin Mary, and in the Middle Ages, mint was used to perfume synagogues.

Spearmint, peppermint, corn mint, and pennyroyal all have, to a greater or lesser degree, a fresh, cleansing aroma and a pleasing flavor. Peppermint is the easiest to grow, requiring only moist soil and some shade to propagate effusively. It is the key ingredient in many sweets and in toothpaste, and as a tea peppermint has a pronounced beneficial effect on a stomachache.

Spearmint is the mint of choice for the mint julep, the great drink of the Antebellum South, which was administered liberally to anyone feeling weak at the knees. To make a julep, you must place about 8 of the tenderest mint leaves you can find into a mixing glass. Add 2 teaspoons of sugar syrup [made by boiling together 2 parts sugar to 1 part water] and bruise the mint leaves with a spoon. Pour in 2 ounces of bourbon and stir gently. Next pour the mixture into a very cold 16-ounce glass [or silver mug, should you have one] filled with shaved ice, and churn it up and down with a spoon. Then add another liberal ounce of bourbon on top and stir the whole with a mint sprig. Recline in a comfortable chair and drink up.

Pennyroyal is primarily used in medicines, rather than in the kitchen, as it has a sharp, somewhat overly pungent taste. It was known to the Romans as *pulegium*, from the Latin *pulex*, meaning "flea," because of its reputed power to kill or drive off that pest. Naturalists of classical times recommended crowns of pennyroyal for those suffering from giddiness.

All the mints were thought to be great inducers of lust and were accounted as witches' herbs, though they were more associated with white magic than black. To the Victorians, however, mint was the symbol of virtue.

Chervil

[ANTHRISCUS CEREFOLIUM, MYRRHIS ODORATA,
OZMORRHIZA LONGISTYLIS ET ALIA]

There are several entirely different plants known as chervil, and though the old herbalists described the herb as "so harmless you cannot use it amiss," modern folks should take care to grow chervil from seed rather than gathering plants from the wild, as some varieties are deadly poison. ¶ The aromatic chervil often called sweet cicely is not recommended for cooking, but, drunk with wine, it was believed to prevent the plague. *Anthriscus cerefolium,* a member of the carrot family, is the chervil featured in the fines herbes of France. The seventeenth-century herbalist Gerard recommended that the roots of this chervil be boiled and dressed with oil and vinegar, "which is very good for old people that are dull and without courage: it rejoiceth and comforteth the heart, and increaseth their lust and strength."

Sorrel

[R U M E X   A C E T O S A]

Sorrel grows in tapering spires of reddish flowers above spear-shaped leaves that change from green in the spring to a deep red in the late summer. Sorrel has always been well received in the kitchen, where its sour leaves add tang to soups and sauces. ¶ In the eighteenth century, sorrel was used to make "verjuice," a drink that also contained vines, leaves, unripe grapes, and crab apples and was taken, inconceivably, to stimulate the appetite. Peasants used to call the herb cuckoo's meat because they believed that cuckoos ate it to clear their throats.

Common sorrel is more of a field flower than a garden flower, as it reseeds itself somewhat too easily for the comfort of its fellow plants. Wood sorrel, which features small white flowers and cloverlike leaves, is not actually sorrel at all but a type of oxalis. Its sour leaves and stem may be the source of its confusion with sorrel.

Sorrel bespeaks parental affection in the language of flowers.

[ANTHEMIS NOBILIS]

Chamomile has been widely used for thousands of years. There is some evidence that the ancient Egyptians employed the herb medicinally, and under the name of *maythen,* it was one of the nine sacred herbs of the Saxons. ¶ Before grass lawns were introduced lawns of chamomile were popular in Renaissance England for their sturdiness and sweet smell; they had the added benefit of requiring mowing only three times a year. In *Henry IV,* Falstaff declares that the more chamomile is trodden upon, the faster it grows, a characteristic that undoubtedly contributed to one of its common names, herb of humility. Sir Francis Drake is reputed to have been playing bowls on a chamomile lawn in Plymouth when the Spanish Armada was sighted offshore; he airily avowed that the Spanish could be defeated after he had finished his game. Its cheerful white flowers and unassuming nature made chamomile a country favorite of the Victorians, to whom it symbolized patience in adversity.

Chamomile's medicinal uses are manifold; it has been applied to every ailment from hysteria to sprained ankles and seems to relieve them all, though it is perhaps best known for its mild sedative effect. Tea made of steeped chamomile flowers has been called the only sure preventative of nightmares. It is also efficacious against nausea and may be given to a fussy baby to relieve colic. An infusion of chamomile flowers; rose petals, hips, and leaves; together with white willow bark can be added to the bath to dispel fatigue. Oil of chamomile, which is a beautiful azure blue when first distilled, is often added to shampoos, as it brings highlights to blonde hair.

Dill

[ANETHUM GRAVEOLENS]

A hardy plant, dill grows happily in cold and temperate climates, sprouting yellow flowers in midsummer that are followed by a profusion of flat seeds. Both the seeds and the spindly leaves are used in cooking.

The name *dill* derives from an old Saxon word meaning "lull," which is exactly what dill does, particularly to babies, who have for generations been fed dill water as a cure for "the frets." Galen, the Greek "Father of Medicine," wrote, "Dill procureth sleep, wherefore garlands of Dill are worn at feasts," which seems strange, since most people like to stay awake while they eat.

In the Middle Ages, dill was reputed to be both a witch preventative and a key ingredient in the cauldron, making it hard to know whether it should be welcomed to or banished from the garden. It is clearly of value in pickling and in making sauces and may cure the hiccups. ¶ In eighteenth-century America, mothers distributed Sabbath-day bouquets of dill, fennel, caraway, and southernwood for their fidgety children to chew during long sermons; accordingly, these herbs were known as "Meetin' Seeds."

Hemp

[CANNIBIS SATIVA]

¶ Officially named Indian hemp, *Cannabis sativa* is the source of much illicit pleasure as well as of wonderfully strong fibers used for rope and cloth, an oil employed in the manufacture of soap and varnish, and birdseed. Though its cultivation is forbidden in the United States, hemp is a valuable commercial crop in China, Russia, and Iran, theoretically for its nonnarcotic by-products.

Hemp's medicinal value has often been tied to its hallucinogenic effects. In Eastern countries the resin was extracted from the plant, mixed with milk or alcohol into a paste, and baked into a cake; the result was called the heavenly guide and the cementer of friendships. Nicholas Culpeper, marching, as usual, to a different drummer, suggested that the juice of the plant, dropped into the ears, "draws forth earwigs or other living creatures." One nickname for the plant is the leaf of delusion, and there was a folk legend that to sleep in a field of hemp was dangerous.

Hemp grows easily. Even in countries where it's illegal, hemp can often be found growing wild by the side of the road, presumably spawned by a stray bit of birdseed. In the garden [should you live in China, Russia, or Iran], hemp has the pleasant property of annihilating all surrounding weeds.

Sage

[S A L V I A S P E C I E S]

Over forty species of sage grow in the United States. All of these attractive plants are a boon to the gardener, as they will grow in dry, inhospitable soils, but only a few sages such as common sage and pineapple sage are welcome in the kitchen, where they are often featured in meat dishes, stuffings, and soups.

Sage's role in the garden and kitchen pale beside its place in the medicine chest. The plant's genus name is derived from the Latin *salvere*, "to save," which points to the herb's curative properties. ¶ From the time of the Roman Empire to the eighteenth century, sage was the preeminent fertility treatment prescribed by physicians, and more than one medico believed that regular doses of sage would ensure long life, if not immortality. As one herbalist wrote, "Why should a man die who has sage in his garden?" In nineteenth-century America, its uses were more prosaic: the leaves of sage were rubbed on the teeth to make them whiter.

Clary sage [*S. sclarea*] is another wonder drug. In medieval Europe it combatted virtually every ill; the name *clary* itself comes from the Latin word for "clear," which points to its efficacy as an eye medication. Clary sage was also a substitute for hops in brewing beer; apparently, sage-brewed alcohol was far more intoxicating than hop-brewed. Today the strong, nutty aroma of clary sage is used by aromatherapists to promote relaxation and dispel anxiety.

For the Victorians sage represented domestic virtue.

Anise

[PIMPINELLA ANISUM]

Anise is most widely known for the licorice flavor its seed imparts to liqueurs such as Pernod and its clandestine cousin absinthe. In addition to these disreputable guises, aniseed is an all-purpose healer, settling to an upset stomach, soothing to a squalling baby, and generally calming to the nerves. So pervasive were its benefits that seventeenth-century herbalists held that anise "had no vice in it." ¶ Anise has also long been regarded as an aphrodisiac, which was probably the foundation of the ancient Roman custom of including an aniseed cake in every wedding feast.

Lemon Verbena

[Lippia citriodora]

Though in the garden lemon verbena has the general appearance of a gangling adolescent, with long limbs sticking out in awkward directions, indoors it is an herb to prize. Its woody, citrus scent can freshen a musty closet or add sparkle to iced tea. ¶ It may even produce improved children; the unknown medieval author of *The Boke of Secretes of Albertus Magnus* suggested hopefully that "infants bearing it shal be very apte to learne and loving learninge and they shal be glad and joyous."

All of the myriad verbenas symbolize sensitivity in floral language.

Valerian

This herb's genus name comes from a Latin word meaning "powerful," which valerian certainly is, particularly as a medicinal plant. Even back in the days when anxiety was mistaken for possession by demons, valerian was prescribed to relieve headaches, tremblings, palpitations, and hysteric complaints. Modern herbalists have dubbed it the Valium of the nineteenth century. Perhaps related is valerian's reputation as a love charm: a girl who decked herself with garlands of valerian would always have lovers, according to peasant wisdom. Furthermore, she would remain unscathed by lightning, as valerian was thought to provide protection in storms. ¶ Witches either love valerian or detest it; the commentators vary in their claims.

Despite its relative adaptability in the garden and its pretty pink or white flowers, valerian is not a common garden plant, probably because it offers up a fairly nasty scent, which earned it the country nickname of phu.

The less potent red valerian is called bloody butcher and bloody fingers in parts of England, which seems less than fair for such a benevolent herb. More reasonably, valerian symbolizes an accommodating disposition in floral language.

Fennel

[F O E N I C U L U M V U L G A R E]

There are many varieties of fennel, all of which are useful from stem to stern, or from root to bud. Its light licorice taste has made its leaves and seeds a favorite flavoring ever since classical times, and the Roman naturalist Pliny avowed that fennel was employed for twenty-two different remedies. However, since he also reported that after snakes had shed their skins, they rubbed themselves against fennel to improve their eyesight, the twenty-two remedies may be viewed with suspicion. ¶ **The Romans were very fond of fennel, laying it under baking bread to spread its fragrance through the dough and mixing the seed into soldiers' rations to improve their strength.** Once cut, however, fennel's feathery leaves wither quickly, and this transience made it a symbol of flattery to the Romans. A relic of this association appears in the Italian expression *dare finocchio*, "to give fennel," which means to flatter.

The early Greeks are known to have eaten the seed in preparation for their Olympic Games, both because of its enlivening properties and because it was thought to promote weight loss. This may have given rise to fennel's meaning for the Victorians: force or strength.

In the Middle Ages, fennel was a valuable safeguard against evil forces. Sprays of fennel and St. John's wort were hung above doors to keep the Devil from entering, and fennel seeds were placed inside keyholes to deter the ingress of ghosts. Poor peasants ate fennel seed to make themselves feel less hungry, and gluttonous noblemen ate it to reduce.

Hyssop

[H Y S S O P U S   O F F I C I N A L I S]

¶ This sweet-smelling herb has been used for cleansing and beautification for centuries. It makes a well-known cameo appearance in Psalm 51, when David, seeking God's forgiveness for his dalliance with Bathsheba, says, "Purge me with hyssop, and I shall be clean; wash me, and I shall be whiter than snow." Though some naysayers caution that the hyssop of the Bible is not our hyssop at all, the herb is still used for purification rituals and consecration ceremonies, which probably engendered hyssop's symbolic meaning: sacrifice.

In the fifteenth and sixteenth centuries, hyssop was a "strewing herb," that is, it was dried and tossed into the corners of a house to dispel bad odors. In the same era, herbalists prescribed six spoonfuls of hyssop juice in a glass of warm ale to improve the complexion.

In Tudor England mazes were sometimes set in hyssop. Hyssop's delightful aroma attracts bees and butterflies as well as people. Its pretty bluish flowers are used for ornamental borders in formal gardens. Hyssop tea and honey are considered delicacies, and hyssop is one of the 130 herbs necessary to make Chartreuse liqueur.

Cinnamon

[CINNAMOMUM ZEYLANICUM]

One of the oldest and most valuable of spices, cinnamon comes from the inner bark of the cinnamon tree, from which it is harvested by an arduous process of peeling and scraping the exterior bark. ¶ It is native to the forests of India and Asia, but it was first brought to the Western world by the Arabs, who sought to conceal the whereabouts of their crop in order to maintain their cinnamon monopoly. This endeavor was foiled by Alexander the Great, whose ships followed the spicy scent of cinnamon wafting forth from the coast of Arabia until they found the trees. The Crusaders brought cinnamon home from the Holy Land and applied it liberally to their foods and love potions.

To the Victorians the cinnamon tree represented forgiveness of injuries.

One Mandrake

[MANDRAGORA SPECIES]

The magical mandrake comes to us so laden with legend and embroidered with extravagance that it's hard to believe that it belongs to the same family as the humble potato [though, in truth, that family contains some of the world's most poisonous vegetation]. Above the ground the mandrake sports large, dark leaves and whitish or purple flowers that turn to yellow berries, but it is the mandrake's subterranean self that led to its remarkable history. Penetrating up to four feet into the earth, the ribbed and knotted mandrake root is often bifurcated like two legs, giving it an unsettling resemblance to a human figure, frequently complete with arms and sexual organs.

¶ As a result, from the dawn of history, the mandrake has been accounted a magical herb, as both a charm for conception and an ingredient in the potions of witches. Its reproductive powers were documented by no less an authority than the Bible's Book of Genesis, in which Rachel and Leah are assisted by the mandrake in bringing forth, respectively, Joseph and Jacob. Not surprisingly, the belief in the mandrake's efficacy as a procreative wonder drug made the herb both sought after and expensive in the medieval era.

Harvesting the mandrake was a delicate business, for supposedly not only did the plant emit hideous shrieks and groans as it was uprooted, but it caused the instantaneous death of the harvester. Great precautions were of course taken: at midnight the mandrake gatherers drew three magic circles around the plant with silver swords. They carefully excavated the plant until it clung to the earth by only a single root. At this excruciating juncture, they tied a rope from the mandrake to a dog and flung a piece of meat just out of the dog's reach; as he lunged for it, the mandrake was pulled out, scream- ing, and the dog fell to the ground, dead. The dangers of retrieving the mandrake made it exceedingly precious and rare, and in the four- teenth and fifteenth centuries, counterfeit mandrake fashioned from sticks flooded the market. Public outrage ensued, and one sixteenth- century writer decried "cheating Knaves and Quacksalvers that carry them around to be sold, therewith to deceive barren women."

In the more sober halls of medicine, the mandrake had been used since classical times as an anesthetic and painkiller before amputations and as a narcotic for those suffering from insomnia and depression. Though a primitive solution, the mandrake probably worked better than most of the other concoctions administered at the time, for the plant does contain hyoscyamine and several other mind-altering alkaloids. In the Mediterranean mandrake berries were thought to strike dumb anyone who ate them; this belief was proba- bly derived from the plant's narcotic effects, and led to a variety of nicknames for mandrake, such as the devil's testicles, the apple of the genie, and the apple of the fool. By the nineteenth century, the belief in the mandrake's magical powers had dissipated, and the herb was relegated to an occasional appearance in an herb garden. Medicinally, it is now little used, science having thankfully developed more efficacious anesthetics.

In the language of flowers, the mandrake is the symbol of rarity.

Catnip

[NEPETA CATARIA]

¶ Catnip, or catmint, is irresistible to cats. Even the most dignified of cats will roll and writhe and generally act drunk when it encounters a bed of catnip. A small pillow filled with dried catnip will induce a milder case of feline euphoria. Rodents, as is fitting for the natural enemy of cats, are said to detest the herb and go to any lengths to avoid it.

The root of the catnip plant is said to make the meek man fierce and the bold downright belligerent. Modern studies show that the herb has a mild hallucinogenic effect when smoked; this may be the source of its reputation for provoking fearlessness.

Unlike most members of the mint family, catnip can prosper in dry and rocky soil. Along with cats, bees are also drawn to the herb.

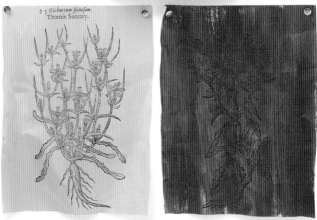

‡ 5 *Cichorium spinosum.*
Thornie Succory.

Chicory

[CICHORIUM INTYBUS, CICHORIUM ENDIVIA]

Chicory is both an emblem of culinary refinement, in its endive and radicchio guises, and a slightly déclassé signal of frugality, when its roots are ground and used as a substitute for coffee. The flowers of chicory are bright blue but notably lazy: they open for four hours a day and not a minute more. ¶ The illustrious Swedish botanist Linnaeus used them in his floral clock because he considered them infallible timekeepers. Oddly enough, when they are placed on an anthill, the blue flowers turn a brilliant red.

Chicory is one of the bitter herbs that God commanded the Israelites to eat with the lamb at Passover. Nonetheless, it was also prescribed by medieval herbalists "for swoonings and passions of the heart."

St. John's Wort

[HYPERICUM PERFORATUM]

Though it will never be cultivated for its beauty, St. John's wort deserves a place in the garden for its many curative and uplifting properties. ¶ A small plant with speckled leaves and yellowish flowers dotted with black, St. John's wort was supposed to have great healing powers by virtue of its associations with Saint John the Baptist, whose blood was represented by the plant's red juice. So profound was the Devil's fear of this herb that it was sometimes called *Fuga daemonium,* "Devil's flight," and it was said that the plant's spotted leaves came from the Devil's attempts to destroy it with a needle. Accordingly, garlands of the herb were hung over windows and doors on the eve of Saint John's Day, when demons were most likely to act up. Haunted houses were cleansed of their undesired astral occupants by having St. John's wort placed underneath the pillows. Sprigs of the herb tucked up over a cradle ensured that the baby within could not be taken for a changeling.

Those untroubled by witches, demons, and sprites might still find St. John's wort valuable for its healing powers. The red juice that so confounded the Devil also led the early herbalists to conclude that the plant was good for healing wounds, "to close them and fill them up." Culpeper recommended it for agues and bruises but particularly for melancholy and madness. This is in accordance with modern herbalists, who find that St. John's wort relieves anxiety and depression.

In the language of flowers, St. John's wort represents animosity, probably due to its unbecoming appearance.

Chili Pepper

[CAPSICUM SPECIES]

Deriving its name from the Greek *kapto*, "I bite," *Capsicum*, or chili pepper, is the source of cayenne pepper, paprika, and other hot-tasting powders. It should not be confused with black pepper, which comes from the berry of an entirely different plant. Native to South America, chili pepper flourishes in temperate and tropical climates, though it may be a successful pot-plant in chillier territories. There are several varieties of *Capsicum* and though all are decorative, not all are edible.

¶ *Capsicum* is primarily known as a spice for food, but it does have a few alternate uses: the pods, powdered and sprinkled inside shoes, make a good foot warmer. Early herbalists believed that hot pepper, eaten with plenty of meat, was a cure for blindness.

[C R O C U S   S A T I V U S]

Precious saffron must be collected by hand from the delicate center of a certain variety of crocus called the true crocus. This lavender flower, which blooms in the autumn, has a tripartite orange stigma at its center. Once dried, these slender, drooping threads are known as saffron and are prized in cooking, cosmetics, and as a coloring or dye. It takes over 75,000 flowers to produce a single pound of saffron, making it the most expensive spice in the world.

¶ The scent of saffron was so beloved by the ancient Romans that their theater seats were strewn with crocus flowers, and saffron-scented water gushed from their fountains. Saffron essence was sprinkled over audiences in Roman amphitheaters to put them in a jovial and receptive mood.

In the Middle Ages, when back-breaking labor was not considered a problem [except, of course, by the people who performed it], saffron was a key ingredient in many recipes. One early cookbook exhorted its readers, "For hen in broth, color it with saffron for Goddes sake." Even today its sweet aroma and warm yellow color make saffron an important element in curries, soups, and stews, and it is indispensable in such specialties as bouillabaisse and paella.

Saffron yields a beautiful yellow dye that is used to color the sacred robes of certain Buddhist sects. In the West, Irish women dyed their children's sheets yellow with saffron; it was thought that the brilliant color would strengthen the limbs of those who lay between the sheets. Saffron is the symbol of mirth in the language of flowers.

[V I S C U M   A L B U M]

There is an old legend that the cross upon which Jesus was crucified was made of mistletoe. As a punishment for lending itself to this use, the shrub was forbidden to grow in the earth and was therefore relegated to a parasitic existence, living on the branches of more virtuous trees. It is still called *herbe de la Croix* in some parts of France.

¶ The ancient Druids believed that mistletoe had magical powers, probably because it grew on the oak tree, which they revered as a gift from heaven. The Roman naturalist Pliny recommended mistletoe as a cure for epilepsy but warned that to be effective, the herb must never touch the ground.

More familiarly, mistletoe provides an excuse for kissing at Christmastime. Hung above a doorway, it creates a free kissing zone on the threshold below. Determined kissers may abandon the convention of the doorway and simply hold a sprig of mistletoe above the head of their intended in order to demand a kiss. One of the common names for mistletoe, by the way, is Kiss-and-Go.

Mistletoe propagates by explosion; the ripe berries burst into the air, sending seeds hurtling toward other branches of the host tree in hopes of finding good homes. Crushed, the berries emit a sticky fluid called birdlime, which is currently used, as Pliny suggested, to cure epilepsy, though the injunction against touching the ground is now disregarded.

In the language of flowers, mistletoe boasts, "I surmount all," probably on account of its lofty habitat.

Goldenrod

[S O L I D A G O   V I R G A U R E A]

Goldenrod sports small, brilliant yellow flowers atop tall, rather ungainly stalks. There are many varieties of goldenrod under the genus name *Solidago,* derived from the Latin *solidare,* "to strengthen," which discloses the medicinal uses of the plant. Goldenrod was much sought after in England in the sixteenth century, when it was a rare and expensive import from America, but when it was discovered growing wild on the Hampstead Heath near London, its popularity declined precipitously, which just goes to show you that trendiness is a centuries-old ailment.

In colonial America goldenrod had a number of different nicknames, including blue mountain tea and woundwort, an unprepossessing moniker that means the herb was used to seal cuts and abrasions. ¶ There is a legend that goldenrod grows where secret treasure is hidden, and witches have been known to use the flowery stalks as divining rods. In the language of flowers, the goldenrod represents encouragement.

List of Herbs

Acknowledgments

For their creativity, energy, and generosity we wish to thank our friends and colleagues: Ann Fiery for writing such smart, insightful, and witty text; Holly Lindem for her gorgeous photography; and Elvis Swift for his distinctive lettering.

Special thanks to Evan Kleiman, who gave graciously of her time and expertise and who introduced us to a host of wonderful people and sources; including Scott Daigre at Hortus, Shirley Kerins at The Huntington Botanical Gardens, Carol Saville, Tom Erd, and Delia Coleman. We would also like to thank Barbara Myers of Scentiments for the glorious flowers.

Jane Field rescued us with last-minute research and props, all from halfway around the world. We are also greatful to Art Gray for his generosity with the additional photography, and Irving Gershenz for his endless energy at the studio. Last but most certainly not least, many, many thanks to Leslie Jonath and Jodi Davis, our editors, for keeping all the bugs out!